Out With Joy

"Ye shall go out with joy and be lead forth in peace"
Isa 55:12

Introduction

    As I write this brief sketch of God's leadership in my life, I want to express that it has been all joy to follow Jesus. It has not always been easy. But, in the center of the circle of God's will there is safety, joy and peace. I met Jesus at age 14, and He has been my Guide, my Strength, my Help, my Provider, my Savior, my Sanctifier, my Friend.

.

In the early 1900's a young married couple, Ambrose Burnside Griffith (b. August 12, 1882; d. April 29, 1956) and Sarah Fox Powell Griffith (b. June 26, 1884; d. March 30, 1952) moved from Pennsylvania to Hunterdon County, New Jersey. Hunterdon is a rolling farm area with stone houses. Today, scented, multicolor roses grow by the road side. Canals and tow roads run parallel to the Delaware River. Stockton, settled in the 1700's, has a six-mile area and a population of about 560. This picturesque area greatly contrasted with the busy

1

rushing cities of the Doylestown and Philadelphia area from which my parents had come.

Sarah and Ambrose were married on April 15, 1903. Into this farm home came joy as well as sorrow. Joy came in welcoming six sons and two daughters: Ambrose Burnside Griffith, Jr born March 24,1904 and died March 29, 1904; Andrew W. born June 18,1905 and died November 1,1906; Edna Elizabeth born August 31, 1909 and died June 1968; William R. born September 14, 1911 and died February 9, 1912; Joseph M. born January 6, 1916 and died March 12, 1917; Elwood George born June 27, 1921and died March 11, 1923. By 1923, the five sons had been laid to rest "Safe in the arms of Jesus." Mother showed me precious remembrances, little ringlets of hair tied with ribbons as she tearfully told of joyous times when one of them had played peakaboo or had done cute little things. They had been happy years yet mixed with much grief.

Some time later they moved from the farm into the village of Stockton, into a two story frame building. My father became an insurance salesman. On July 30, 1922, Harold Le Roy was born. On Novembe 30, 1923, I joined the family, which then included my parents and two siblings, Edna and Harold.

I do not know why they moved to Camden, NJ unless it was to be closer to family members or to a more populated area for insurance sales. Nevertheless we purchased and moved into a newly constructed two-story three bedroom brick home in May of 1924. Edna Elizabeth Griffith, my older and only sister, attended high school at the time. My mother, a homemaker, devoted her time to her family. My father continued to sell insurance. He did well and became a district manager for Metropolitan Insurance.

Let me recount one interesting story I heard as a child. It happened soon after we had moved to Camden. Edna, a high school senior, walked the several miles to

Camden High.   One day the family became worried. Edna had not arrived home as expected.   About dusk an exhausted Edna arrived. She had walked and walked. But the farther she went the less familiar things seemed. The number, 929,   should have been home. But it was not home! Edna then realized she was lost!   What should she do?   In frustration and almost panic she looked around.   She saw the street sign, South Fourth Street. Immediately this country kid knew what she had done. She had gone to the 900's of South Fourth Street instead of to 929 North Fourth where we lived. She got her extra miles in that day! She saw more of Camden than any other member of the family! She never made that mistake again!

My curiosity was evident at an early age! My first remembered exploit was pulling rubber tubes out from under Edna's piano. I must have been near age three. I crawled under the keyboard of the Lester player piano. It was very interesting. I saw lots of little rubber tubes

4

and examined them one by one. I pulled one of them out! It was fun, so I pulled out some more. My mother discovered me! I was in big trouble! The piano no longer played the cylinders of sheet music! This was a very expensive exploration in more than one way!

When the financial crash came in 1930 no one bought insurance. It was difficult to buy necessities. My father became a jack of all trades. He painted houses, fixed furnaces, even sold cars for a while. He just worked at whatever he could find. We never received government welfare and we never went hungry, but we had hand-me-down clothes and lived frugally. My mother sewed and fixed these hand-me-downs until we always looked nice. My father bought rubber soles at the five and ten cent store and glued them on to our shoes. We bought bread at a day old bakery. We did many things to conserve. However, we felt rich when we got a five cent ice cream cone and even richer if we had another penny to get "jimmies" on it (now called sprinkles, little chocolate pieces).   And really, we did not know we were poor. We were happy and God always made a way and provided for us.

One day while I was with my father in the five and ten cent store, I saw shoe cleats and wanted them.   I wanted my heals to go clickety-clack.   Other kids had them. My dad said, "No." But I slipped around when he was not looking and put a pair in my pocket.   Later at home I tried to nail them on my shoe heels. My dad saw this!   He instructed me to return them and tell the clerk that I had stolen them. We went immediately back to the store. I was humiliated, ashamed and cured! My parents, though not professing Christians, taught us principles of character and honesty.

Some of my earliest memories are connected with State Street Methodist Episcopal Church. It was a large and friendly church. The saints impacted my life as they encouraged me to serve the Lord. Names I recall include Mrs. Daisy Stevenson, Mr Frank Patterson, Mr and Mrs.

Earl Harris, Mrs. Gladys Richman, Mr and Mrs. Charles Richman, Mr and Mrs Jim Baxter. Also I remember the Choir director, Mr Clinton Lowden, and the organist, Myrtle Perkins.   There were many more. Five hundred attended Sunday School, including me,

I have early memories of singing in the children's choir.   We marched across the back of the sanctuary and up the center aisle in our black and white choir robes carrying the Methodist Hymnal singing ---

"Holy, Holy, Holy Lord God Almighty!

Early in the morning our song shall rise to Thee.

Holy, Holy, Holy! Merciful and Mighty!

God in three Persons, blessed Trinity!

We reverently stood inside the altar with bowed heads during the pastoral prayer and then we sang our special number.   In the singing of the great Methodist hymns there was born in my heart a desire to know God to love and serve Him. I could not have been more than seven or eight years old at this time. My pastor, Rev. G. W. Hanners, always gave a children's sermon. He came down and stood in front of where we sat. Truth began changes in my heart.

During my time in the Junior department of the Sunday School, Mrs. Mary Richmond, a precious older saint of God, presented missionary stories. Her testimony of God's leadership in her life created in my heart a hunger for spiritural things. I did not get saved then, but I began Scripture memorization that paid dividends later, memorizing the Ten Commandments and the Books of the Old and New Testaments. Prizes were given for reciting these in front of the Junior Department Sunday School. I was a timid child but somehow did this.

My brother and I became young entrepreneurs. We grew up during the depression years of the thirties. We learned the value of a good work ethic and tried to earn money to help buy our clothing. In the hot summer, during the ball games at the Pine Point Park, we sold

8

snowballs. Harold used his wagon, purchased a block of ice, and we were in business. He scraped the ice to make the "snow balls." My mother made the various flavors to put on the snow balls-- cherry, root-beer, chocolate, and several others. I put the flavors on and collected the money. We sold three sizes 5 cent, 10 cent and 15 cent ones. Who didn't want a snowball on a hot summer day?

We also sold Easter eggs. There was a small candy factory near our home. We bought a box of 100 small Easter eggs for $.60 and sold them 1 cent each and had 40% profit. We took orders for the fancy decorated ones.

A great deal of credit for my being a Christian goes to Edna, my sister. At age 20 she graduated with honors from the University of Pennsylvania. She started to teach school about the time I started kindergarten. Mr. Timberlake, the janitor, at Hatch Jr. High, where Edna

9

taught, talked   to her about her soul. As a result of his testimony and influence she was saved. Later she became the religious education director at the Wiley Methodist Episcopal Church, located at Third and Beckett Street. Not long after this, Edna gave me my first Bible and encouraged me to read it through in a year, suggesting that I read three chapters a day and five on Sunday. I've done this many times since. She also encouraged me to tithe, which I have always done, even when I had very little.

School, plus basket ball games,   football games, my   hockey team, and swimming club occupied my time. It was easy to miss a few Sunday school sessions. But I had a Sunday school teacher who was   faithful to me. When I missed, my teacher was at our front door sweetly urging me to be in Sunday school.   My mother said to me, "We won't have your teacher coming back. You will go to Sunday school."

During the first revival I ever attended, about 1937, I came under deep conviction for sin.   Rev. and

Mrs. Jarrett Aycock, Nazarene evangelists, preached this revival at State Street Methodist Church. I became a seeker, knelt at the altar and repented of my sins. Mrs. Aycock knelt beside me to pray and guided me into the kingdom. Thank God, His mercy reached me and His grace brought forgiveness. From this time on I attended church every Sunday morning and evening. The Wednesday prayer service became important even though I was the only youth there. I grew to know the saints at State Street and grew in grace and in knowledge of the Lord.

In order to become a member of the church, I enrolled in the Church Membership Class. We studied the youth catechism and learned the Wesleyan doctrines. Pastor Rev. Edward A. Chambers, was very helpful. He encouraged me to teach Sunday School. At age 14, I taught my first class of nine second grade boys. The following summer from 9:00 am. to 11:30 am., I taught about twenty beginners in our two-week Vacation Bible

11

School.

The pastor and leaders of the church were interested in helping me become a lay leader. For several years they arranged for me to go to four or five Methodist Teacher Training sessions and receive certification. Already God was getting me ready for what I love best-- teaching His Word.

Our Epworth League had a Bible contest about the time I was 16. We were given a question each week and were to bring the answer the next Sunday. Edna had Bible dictionaries and study books. I used them and won the contest. The prize was a fully paid week at Pennington Institute Youth Camp. This was my first time ever away from home for overnight. God was getting this backward timid girl ready for His will. I went and did very well even with some homesickness. During the camp I took a course of study in home missions. The camp ended with an impressive campfire service. All to whom God had spoken were requested to throw a fagot into the fire, symbolizing our desire to spread the light of, truth to others. At that time, God called me to His service to be a missionary to Kentucky. With purpose and challenge I threw my fagot into the fire. This new purpose to do the will of God gave direction to my life. I testified to my call to Kentucky home missions. Many discouraging things came to hinder. One person told me, "You'll soon forget that." But what the Holy Spirit speaks becomes as fire to the soul.

Other early memories are connected with our summer home built in Pleasantville, New Jersey. My mother tells me that they did not have a bed for me at this time (1924) so pulled out a dresser drawer put a pillow in it and me. Our summer home was located on Lake's Bay about 150 feet from the water's edge. One could stand in our yard and look across the six-mile bay and see the lights of Atlantic City, Longport, Margate, and Ocean City. Occasionally during the flood tides or when strong northeastern storms came, we tied a boat at our front porch.   Harold and I enjoyed this, but my mother did not think it was so great.

We were early instructed not to go near the boats and the water unless with an adult. But kids are kids, and when Harold and I were about five or six year old, we fell over board. We knew we were in trouble. We helped each other get out, but we did not go near the house. Instead we hid behind the tool shed until our clothes were dry.

We always had a couple of boats, a small row boat and a motor/sail boat. My brother and I spent much time sailing,   fishing, crabbing, swimming and occasionally clamming.   As soon as school was out for the summer my father took us down to stay at our summer home and he commuted.   He came on Friday evening and always brought produce and fruit from the New Jersey garden farms. On Saturdays, Dad, Harold and I often would get up early, sometimes at 4:30 or 5:00 am., "to catch the tide" as my dad would say. We went across Lakes Bay to find a good fishing spot. When the tide began to turn, we moved and found a good place to catch crabs. My dear mother never went with us. She had a fear of the water. She preferred to stay at home. Sometimes my Aunt Lizzie, who lived in Pleasantville, would come down and spend the day with her. Other times my mother would go to her house. But we could always count on mother to be there when we returned, and to have a meal ready for us. She always had a large kettle of water on to cook the crabs. Crabs were dumped alive into boiling water seasoned with old bay and vinegar.

While we were in Pleasantville I found a church home for the summer. St. John's Methodist Protestant Church was located about two miles from us. I met new Christian friends and enjoyed fellowship. In fact my first memories of understanding heart holiness were from a tract given to me by a lay preacher, Claude Mathis from St John's Church.

Harold went to Woodrow Wilson High School.

His interest was business and shop. Later he went to Wharton School of Business which was a part of the University of Pennsylvania.

Edna and I went to Camden High School. She graduated and went on to the University of Pennsylvania to graduate in 1930 with honors. She began her teaching career about the time Harold and I   started   Read Elementary School at 5th Street and York. When Harold started school I cried and begged to go even though I was only four years old.   Finally the kindergarten teacher said, "let her come." My formal education began at age 4 years. I loved every minute of it! Miss McDonald, my teacher, was special to me. We marched, played and learned. I remember carrying the American flag or the little triangle and playing it in the rhythm band.   New Jersey law required that I be six years of age before entering first grade so I stayed in kindergarten for one and a half years.   Every thing we did was fun and I did not mind staying. However, in January of 1930, Miss Hagen became my first grade teacher. I tried to imitate her stately walk. I loved school and loved my teachers.

Edna's work as Christian Education Director brought me in to contact with Wiley Methodist Church and the Wiley Mission family. It gave me opportunity to know more Christian young people and to go to camp meeting services. Laura Gilmore Foreman became a lifelong and close friend. I learned more about consecration and purity of heart from the preaching and friends at Wiley. Each summer I attended the Wiley Mission Camp Meetings. I heard some of the choice holiness preachers of the late thirties and forties.

School passed rapidly and then came graduation from high school in January 1942. In December 1941 the Japanese bombed Pearl Harbor. I graduated into a war torn world. My brother enlisted. So did other friends. Our world was changed.

Early College Training

I wanted to go to Asbury College, in KY. My folks

said, "If you go to University of Pennsylvania we'll help you." They had sacrificed to help Edna graduate from Penn. She had ridden the ferry to Philadelphia and, walked many miles to the university to complete her degree in 1930. But God had given me a call into full time Christian work. I felt I wanted to go to a Christian college. Perhaps I should back up. I knew of Asbury College because our church had an evangelist, Dr. O. H. McCrary who lived in Wilmore, KY. Edna encouraged me to go. Others did.... but interesting and providentially, Sunny McCrary, Dr. O. H. McCrary's daughter became my big sister when I arrived at Asbury College.

While in my last two years of high school, I worked on the week-ends in a W.T. Grant store. After graduation I began as a full time worker and was placed in charge of the Domestic department. Work hours were from 9:00 am. to 5:00 pm. Monday through Friday and 9:00 to 9:00 on Saturday. The work was enjoyable, but it was merely a stepping stone to get to college.

18

In January 1942 I enrolled in night classes at the College of South Jersey & South Jersey Law School which later became a part of Rutgers. A full college load meant going to school from 6:00 pm. to 10 pm. five nights a week. By the summer of 1943, I had finished. . .

By September of 1943 I had saved enough money to enter Asbury College as a Junior All of my credits transferred. During my first semester I had a housekeeping job cleaning Glide/Crawford parlor. After meeting Miss Ruth VanSciver, the college librarian, I transferred to work in the college library, opening the library at 7:30a,.m. and closing at 10 p.m.. All my free time up to eight hours a day was spent working in the library. The student pay at that time was twenty-five cents an hour. It took courage to ask Dr. Z. T. Johnson for a pay increase. But since I worked 8 hours each day I felt I deserved more than student pay rate. Minimum wage at that time was seventy-five cents an hour. He agreed and

I received fifty cents an hour conditioned on the basis that I would not tell the other students my pay rate.

God helped me meet all my financial obligations. I hated debt, so did not borrow money. However, at the end of my junior year, my meal tickets were all spent and my cash was gone. I told no one of my need. I lived on a jar of jelly and a package of buns which lasted me about a week. My railroad ticket got me home to NJ. The 21 hour train ride was a time of fasting. I did not have a weight problem then! I never told anyone about this until years later.

While at Asbury I learned more about leaning on God's Word and how foolish it was to lean on my own understanding. God spoke,

> *"He it is that loveth me; and he that loveth*
> *me shall be loved of my Father and I will*
> *love him and will manifest myself to him."*
>
> *John 14 :21*

My Christian Service appointment while at

Asbury included working at Davis Bottoms, a slum area of Lexington. God gave me a burden for souls and lots of practical experience as we called in the homes and ministered. At Thanksgiving time we prepared a turkey dinner with all the "fixin's" and served it to a large group of these people. The work we began later became a Methodist Mission called Nathaniel Chapel; it is located on DeRhode Street and still operates today.

Involvement in the Mountain Missionary Prayer Band and the Student Volunteer Prayer Group brought me in contact with the Kentucky Mountain Holiness Association. I visited and preached at Mt Carmel High School. My text from Exodus 33:15 "My *presence shall go with thee and I will give you rest.*" I spoke about the privileges, joy, and rest in living in God's Presence. God blessed in this service as several came to the altar. I began to sense God's leadership for my life. I wanted to teach in a Bible College but I greatly feared "living by faith." I had a strong work ethic and had become in one sense a workaholic. How could one live by faith? You had to earn a living!

God gave me His **Word of promise** to overcome my fears and reasonings!   The Word of God quickened to me during these days of struggle became **my life verse**. Isa. 55:12-13

"You shall go out with joy and be lead forth

in peace, the hills and mountains will break

forth into singing and all the trees of

the field shall clap their hands. Instead

of the thorn shall come up the fir tree and

instead of the briar will grow up the myrtle:

and it shall be to the Lord for a name, for

an everlasting sign that shall not be cut off."

Each year Asbury College had Dr. Lela G. McConnell, president and founder of KMHA, speak in the college chapel. In the fall of 1945, as President of the Mountain Missionary Society, it was my responsibility to be in charge of that chapel service, introduce the speaker and receive the offering for the Kentucky Mountain Holiness Association. The group was delayed in arriving on campus due to a flat tire. I missed my study hours waiting for them. In fulfilling my responsibilities with the chapel I was late for class. We had a test in Physiology. I failed! No retakes were possible. My only "F" ever! However, I did pass the course.

When my good friend, Asbury student Meredythe Scheflen, and I visited Mt Carmel, we stayed in the guest room at Dr Lela G. McConnell's cottage. (Meredythe was an outstanding missionary and educator in Bolivia for more than fifty years.) The plan was to get up early and go out to enjoy the hills during our morning devotions. Merry, the sleepyhead, refused to get up. I tried to help her by pulling off her covers. The sheet tore almost in two! What an embarrassment! What could I do? Neither of us had money to replace it. How could we confess such a deed?

The next week Miss Ruth VanSciver, the Asbury College librarian and a close friend to both of us, had an extra sheet come back with her laundry. She never found an owner! We sent "the sheet" to Mt Carmel to pay for the torn one. We never did find anyone with a missing sheet. God took care in His own special way.

During my senior year Rev. John Lewis from the Methodist Mountain Mission contacted me about working with the Methodist Mission Group either in eastern Kentucky or in western Kentucky at Henderson Settlement. I asked Rev. Lewis if my co-workers would be holiness people and would I be free to teach and preach the doctrine. He assured me that I could teach it but not all the co-workers would feel as I did. That settled it for me. I wanted to be with a true holiness group.

In 1945 after graduation from Asbury College I continued to work at the college library and prepared to go to Seminary to begin my Masters degree. I entered

Asbury Theological Seminary in the fall of 1945. I completed all my studies except for one quarter and my thesis. I needed money to continue in school. I returned to New Jersey and soon had a job working in the office of a tug boat company. In late July a teaching position opened in south eastern Kentucky; I immediately took it. It was for me another step in answering my call. In August 1946, I began to teach school in McCreary County, Kentucky.

The school was located at a place called Bald Knob. Someone said it was so far back that if you went any further you were coming out on the other side. One could get there by a dirt road that was impassable in winter or by traveling on the Sterns Line coal miner's train. Today this same trip is a tourist attraction out of Sterns, KY. The train left at 5:00 A.M.. in the morning to carry the miners to their places of labor. It stopped at several places where miners could get off and walk to the various mines.

Arrangements were made for me to live with one of

the coal miners' families. The King home was full. They had eight children. They fixed a shed for me to live in, and one of their girls stayed with me each night. This-- "my home"-- was a little different! I had come from a home with central heat; now I had a coal stove in the center of my "one room house." I had never built a fire! I soon learned! I used a coal stove for heat and for cooking. If I did not get up in the night and add fuel I had to melt the ice in the morning to wash my face. I faced the challenges knowing that God had called me to Kentucky and knowing that I would gain experience and love for the people.

On many week ends I went out to Whitley City and stayed with friends, Rev. and Mrs. Walter Piper. "Pappy and Mammy Piper" opened their Methodist parsonage home for me and another teacher friend, Frances Slozat. We helped in the Sunday School, and I preached a few times. On Monday at 4:30 A.M. Papa Piper took us to Sterns, Kentucky, where we could get the coal miners' train. I got off at Blue Heron which was just a stop and walked a half mile to the commissary mine store. One of my eighth graders met me, and we walked a rugged couple of miles up hill to the school house. The same boy built the fires for me at the school house.

Here I was a city girl (Camden/Philadelphia area), where we had two or three rooms for one grade, now faced with 65 students and all eight grades in one room. Thirteen of the little ones could not write their names; the eighth grade boys were taller than I.

I was an inveterate reader and "Tom Brown's School Days" gave me some idea of how to handle this rural school. The students helped formulate the rules and penalties. We wrote them on the blackboard. At recess I joined them to play and learned some of their games and taught them some of mine. Many of the parents invited me for meals. I visited in the homes of every one of my students. Early in the year one very small boy who left home in the dark in order to get to school on time fell asleep and fell out of his chair. I picked him up comforted him and dried his tears. It was his father who sent me a paddle with air holes and said, "Use it or they won't learn." I used the paddle about twice on two of the bigger boys but never had to again.

On one occasion we planned a box auction. The girls made pies and put them in beautifully decorated boxes. The boys bid for the pies with the privilege of eating with the girls. One of the fathers auctioned for us. We raise several hundred dollars to purchase library books for the school. The eighth grade boy who bought my pie was too timid to eat with me, but I gladly shared with him. The whole community turned out for this time of fun and fellowship. I completed the year with many of the parents pleased with the progress of their children.

During this time I made other friendships that have lasted through the years--   Fannie Morgan, the secretary to the County Superintendent, her sister, Nanny, and niece Betty Jo Olson. I was young and full of fun and Nanny

28

use to say, "You put on your pharisaical robe to go to church." Betty Jo, her daughter, was just a child then but has told me several times in recent years how my life influenced her to be a Christian. God placed me there for just a year to accomplish His will and to teach me lessons I needed.

In the fall of 1947 enrollment in Kentucky Mountain Bible Institute was next. I needed more Bible training and I wanted to know more about this matter of "living by faith." My curriculum consisted primarily of Bible and theology courses. During this school year, God helped me to say that last "yes" to His will, and He sanctified my soul. I knew that I was totally God's and that all my life was to be a love offering poured out in His service and for His glory. His people were my people and His will my desire. The verse that Rev. Martha L. Archer gave me along with my diploma in May of 1948 was -- *"For God has not given us the spirit of fear; but of power, and of love, and of a sound mind"* (2 Timothy 1:7)

Early Ministry in the KMHA

In the May 1948 KMHA Conference, Dr. Lela G. McConnell assigned me to be an assistant pastor with Rev. Eunice Kirk. Our assignment was Jett's Creek, a community that had no electricity or even a road. We traveled the creek bed and banks.

After conference, someone took us out to the county line, Owsley/Breathitt, on Highway 30, pointed to a path and said "that is the way to Jetts Creek." Eunice and I climbed up on the ridge, walked a few feet and then the path led through the woods and out and down a steep, and I mean steep, steep, steep winding way. There were no trees on that hillside. I was carrying a suitcase and a portable typewriter. I lost my footing, the suitcase went one way, the typewriter another as I fell and slid down the hill grabbing for rocks, or whatever to stop my plunge. At the bottom I picked myself up and gathered together my things. This was my introduction to Jett's Creek!

Miss Kirk and I lived in a small frame house at the head of the hollow. We served two communities, Jett's Creek and

Mill Branch. On Sunday, my job was to go to the pasture and find Beauty, the horse, and saddle her. I'd never been near a horse! But I quickly learned to find Beauty and saddle her. She was gentle and friendly.

Two of us on one horse rode to the school house, held Sunday school and church; washed our hands in the creek, ate our sack lunch and rode horseback several miles over the rugged hills to Mill Branch school house. One place the path was so steep that the men, I was told, got off and led their horses down. But we rode over it!

Arriving at Mill Branch school house, in Lee County we had Sunday school and church. We visited homes till late afternoon. We usually stayed all night in a different home each week-end, had supper there and then an evening service in that home. The homes were small and sometimes we slept in the same room with the host and hostess. On one occasion I was awakened in the night by hushed voices. I listened and wondered! Miss Kirk later said "They were bootlegging." I learned that making alcoholic beverages is "moonshine-ing"

31

but illegal selling is "bootlegging."

The next morning we rode to the school house and had children's meeting before returning home. We tried to have as many services as possible while at Mill Branch.

This was all new to me. My heart was thrilled and I loved what I was doing. I found God's inexhaustible resources were mine. *"The joy of the Lord,"was my strength.*

The city girl had much to learn. I learned to carpenter by building steps into our parsonage home. These replaced the large rocks that substituted for steps. Later I built a book shelf. Our outhouse was falling over, so I sent word to Mr Raymond Swauger, at Mt Carmel, of our need. He pre-fabbed a toilet for us. When the lumber arrived I built the new outhouse. Miss Kirk was truly a pioneer. I was becoming one! I also learned to love and appreciate the good people of eastern Kentucky. They provided us with milk, and vegetables from their gardens. We had gracious fellowship in their homes.

Let me pause-- to tell a bit about Rev Eunice Kirk, a

32

KMHA pioneer pastor who was my co-worker on this first assignment. She was extremely frugal to the point that it became a joke. Jett's Creek had no electricity. We cooked on an oil stove.

The stove had a leak in the pipe. We could not leave the tank of oil on all the tme. Eunice would not waste oil! When we cooked supper and had taken the tank off, to use up the oil in the stove she cooked her oatmeal for the next day. I could not eat cold and lumpy oatmeal.

I drank coffee: she did not, but thought it extravagant and said, "What will the neighbors think if they smell coffee at our house. You'll have to pay for it yourself." Later we were in Jackson shopping and I sggested we have an ice cream cone. Her response, "That is your dessert for supper."

Another incident of frugality and creativity-- We lighted with an Aladdin lamp. They provided good lighting and for us a place to cook. We held a very small skillet over the lamp to fry eggs!

I add while Eunice Kirk was hard on her self she was very generous with others. She bought shoes and clothes for the children of a co-worker.

Eunice Kirk was a servant pastor and well known in several counties in Eastern KY. This story she told one conference. She had everyone in stitches they laughed so hard. It was dark as she traveled home from a pastoral call. She dropped her glasses. She could not find them even by crawling on hands and knees searching. She knew she could not go and leave them. They could be stepped on and broken   After a long search what could she do?   She would just stay until morning. How many of us would do that?   She curled up under the tree and piled leaves on to keep warm, waited until day light and found her glasses! She laughed and entertained the whole conference with this testimony.

The youth loved and respected her. At her decease a high school lad came to her funeral. He placed a small card in her casket. It was rumpled and yellow. He said as he placed it, "This is a pledge card she had us sign in red ink, promising God we would never drink any alcoholic beverages. I signed it when I was 6 years old and have kept my promise. Miss Kirk was my teacher and friend."

During that summer, my sister and brother-in-law, Edna and Rev. John Delamater, visited me at Jett's Creek.. John was thrilled with the beauty of the hills. He exclaimed, "If I were a young man this is where I'd like to be." He was not a young man and not being use to walking along the creeks and slippery rocks he slid and sat in the creek. Water and mud did not take his joy. He arose unhurt, laughed and trudged on. My sister worried about his good navy blue suit. But their joy in the Lord was above material things. When we arrived at the parsonage he sat on the porch and enjoyed the rugged beauty of eastern Kentucky.

In the fall of 1948, I moved to Lee County to teach at the Tallega Mission Elementary School and continued to pastor at Mill Branch. I rode horseback or walked the three miles along the Middle Fork of the Kentucky River to Mill Branch. On one occasion I had a horse that was not accustomed to women riding it. The horse tried to throw me! It pranced and danced around on its hind feet! I thought I would end up in the river which ran close to the path! And if not in the river at least on a lonely path with broken bones! It was a path not too many people traveled.

Rev. Marvin Wheeler had told me what to do if the horse ever acted like this. I pulled up on the reins and said with authority, "Come up here, Dubby," as I kicked the horse in his sides. When Dubby settled on all fours, I quickly got off! I had enough! I led him back to the barn. I preferred to walk the three miles and arrive safely.

In the Tallega elementary school we enrolled over 60 students. Mrs. Marie Davis taught the lower grades, I taught the fourth grade through the eighth. Rev. and Mrs.(Frances) Marvin Wheeler pastored the Tallega

Church. God prospered and blessed us in this ministry. We saw fruit for our labor through our school chapels and in the lives of our students, some fruit even many years later. We gained many new friends in the Lord. When the school year ended, I returned to New Jersey. I wanted to finish my Masters degree at Asbury Theological Seminary and needed money.

I had a friend who worked for the Lumberman's Mutual Insurance Company. She helped me get a job. The office was located on the 12th floor of the PSFS Building at 13th and Market Street in Philadelphia. After one year working, I returned to Asbury Seminary for my last quarter. My Master's Thesis, an interesting subject, was "The History of Christian Education in the Kentucky Mountains." A copy of it is in KMBC Library.

It was a joy to have Elma Reed and Mary Swartwout come to my graduation in 1950 with the purpose to bring me back to the KMHA.

The plan was for me to teach at the Kentucky

Mountain Bible Institute. Dr McConnell sent word that she wanted me to prepare to be the next librarian at KMBI. I needed more hours to do this. I spent part of the summer of 1950 at the University of Kentucky taking nine hours of credit in Library Science. A big order and difficult weeks. In the Reference/Bibliography course we needed a working acquaintance with 300 reference books . God opened opportunity for me to work in the University Library and gain good experience,

In the fall Dr McConnell needed an English teacher at Mt Carmel. Classes had already started when I arrived on the Bible school campus thinking I had a week to get settled before school started. A phone call instructed me that I was needed more at Mt Carmel than at KMBI. Dr. McConnell handed me my teaching materials-- two freshmen English classes, two sophomore English classes, a geometry class and a speech class. I taught the next day! This was for the school year 1950- 51.

Radio Station WMTC (Winning Men To Christ)

began in 1948, In the early days there were many local school programs aired weekly. The teachers from the county schools brought their students to the studio to present a variety of programs. The kids were scared but loved it. It was publicity for the KMHA , Mt Carmel, and the county schools.

At that time I taught geometry at Mt Carmel. We presented a 15 minute program telling all the uses of geometry in the home and ended by singing, "I love geometry because it is so easy to learn."

Ministry at Kentucky Mountain Bible College

In the fall of 1951 I was released to go to KMBI to teach. Miss McConnell said, "Pray in someone to take your place here at Mt Carmel." John Andrus came and I was free to go to KMBI.

When I first came there were two main buildings, the Administration Building and Myers Chapel. The ladies dorm was in the Ad building above the offices, dining room, library and classrooms. The Fisher family (two children at that time) and young men lived in Myers Hall above the chapel.

There was a two car garage building next to Myers Hall with a gasoline pump. The only campus car was parked there and the other half was used for repairing equipment. What excitement when someone stepped on the gas heater pipe to reach and turn on the gasoline pump! The pipe broke and fire shot out! The greasy floor was aflame! Someone ran to get the car out of the other stall. Other ran with fire extinguishers! The whole student body appeared to help. The fire was soon extinguished without a great deal of damage.

Swauger Hall was built about 1953. It became the dining Hall, kitchen and pantry. There was also a faculty/staff kitchen used for 3:00 p.m. coffee and fellowship. The second and third floors became the new men's dorm.

Early in the sixties a decision was made to put a full

basement under the Administration Building. Originally there was a laundry and one classroom at the south end. There was a small potato and fruit cellar storage.

Dr. Karl Paulo, Gene Light, and Clifford Richards engineered this feat. The entire building 30'60" wide 85' long was raised on jacks and rail road ties. A small bulldozer cleared out the dirt under the major part of the building. People lived in the building while the work continued. What a feat! Summer storms and wind came! Prayer went up! Without incident the work was finished! Considering the the size of the building and the limited equipment available at the time, one marvels at the wisdom God gives! There were no work teams in that day.

Dr McConnell always said, "if we do maintenance work, dig a ditch, fix a car, cook, preach, teach or whatever, it is all for the advance of this holiness work. Every one is important!

It was not long until Brengle Building was under

construction. Part of the building rests on a large rock foundation. However, a stream runs thru part of it and a large conduit carries the water west. It was completed in 1955 Brengle is a large "L" shaped building that houses a large dining room that seats 140 people and includes kitchen and pantry. The second and third floor houses the young men. The music department was located on the ground level with practice rooms for piano and organ as well as teacher studios and music classroom.

Miss Celia Gibson and I became Swauger Hall supervisors for the girls .and I remained in that capacity along with my teaching until 1990. Miss Celia Gibson was also the librarian.

My work began as a Christian Education and Bible teacher I also had two radio programs on WMTC Radio Station, fifteen minute daily travel-log and a thirty minute Bible study on Saturdays.

For several years I was assistant to Miss Celia Gibson in   the library and was part of the Library committee. Later when Miss Celia Gibson retired and Ava Smith and others came to help, I received an appointment to chair the Library Committee. I never did become the librarian, even though I had prepared for it. My heart was more in the classroom. Soon I was teaching a full load, inluding Bible, theology and Christian Education.

During my first year (1950-51) of teaching at KMBC I received word that my mother had a cerebral hemorrhage. She and my dad were on their way home from Florida. I traveled by bus to Manning, South Carolina, to be with her. She died Palm Sunday morning, March 30, at the age of 68. I drove my father home to NJ. This was a very difficult time I was very close to my mother, God gave me comfort thru His Word.

"Blessed be God, even the Father of our Lord Jesus Christ, the Father of mercies and the God of all comfort: who comforteth us in all our tribulations that we may be able to comfort them

43

which are in any trouble by the comfort wherewith
we ourselves are comforted." 1 Cor. 1:2-3

Even before I moved to KMBI to teach, I began ministry with the student pastorates. Students were given practical Christian service in the KMHA churches and in local school houses. Mrs Nettie Myers was the director of Christian Service. Students held Sunday school and church in the school houses at Mill Branch, Little Frozen, Coal Branch, Sandy Ridge, Rose Fork, Johnson Fork and other places. With a faculty or staff member to train or guide them, they were responsible for the full ministry of the church. This responsibility included the finances, the Christmas, Rally Day, Easter, and Children's day programs as well as revivals. The students received practical training.

Before too many years, Mrs. Myers needed an assistant. By 1960 I had been appointed as the Director of the Christian Service Department. This I did for about 40 years or until 2000. We enlarged this ministry as we moved into accreditation with AABC. I attended Christian Service Personnel Conferences sponsored by AABC We implemented. many improvements. AABC complimented us on the fine Christian Service Department, stating that it surpassed that of some larger schools. To God be the glory!

I served a two year term as President of KMBC Alumni Association in the seventies. The Alumni Project completed during that time was the blacktop of the main campus roads, at a cost of $20,000. The first donation on this first black top project was given by Mr and Mrs Thomas. They visited their daughter Mrs Naomi Card '60 often and were well aware of the clouds of dust that arose from the gravel. We sold so many square feet of black top until we reach the amount needed.

As the school grew and buildings increased, additional blacktop was continued until the whole campus and up the hill to the residences had been black topped.

45

In the early years, "The Mountain Top Echo" was printed occasionally. Around 1951 a group of us got the idea we needed an Alumni Paper printed quarterly.. Alice Pettit '49 suggested a name "News and Do's." We liked that and voted for that name. I was appoined the first Editor in 1951 and continued involvement for about 10 or 12 years.

During nine summers beginning in 1960 I traveled for the Kentuky Mountain Holiness Association in deputation services. I traveled with Miss Genelle Day and various trios and singing groups. What a priviledge to speak for the Lord and to meet so many of our constituents and see so much country. One year we went to the west coast, Church people loved our students, their clear testimonies and singing.

When I came we had one course in Christian Education, Child evangelism. My main ministry was to develop the Christian Education Department. We soon had a full curriculum which I designed for training in church ministry for all ages. It included Introduction to to Christian Education, Child Development, and Teaching Elementary Bible, Principles and Methods of Teaching, Christian Education for each age group-- adults, children, youth.   The curriculum also included Leadership and Administration, including delegation, conducting board meetings, and time management for Christian Education Directors .

In 2000, we launched the CE Elementary Teacher Education Program which grants certification for teaching in Christian Day Schools.   In the process of preparing the curriculum, I visited the Denver, Colorado Office of Association of Christian Schools International. Dr. Merry Gunnell, the ACSI Schools Advisor was well pleased with our curriculum plans.

While my major was in Christian Education, I was qualified and taught in the areas of Theology and Bible. In my early years I taught more of the theoogy classes The students joked saying, "We take Griffith theology."

My hope and joy has been to see students grasp truth and walk in the light of it.

I have found delight in counseling the girls in the dorm., at the altar, and in the classroom. Dorm supervising was a joy for me from 1954 until 1990. We shared many times of happiness and fun together. Dorm life included Saturday night parties. Each staff was given steak when they butchered at the farm. Mary Ellen Mowery and I saved ours and shared with the girls. We put the desks from each room end to end in the 2nd floor hall. . The students provided what they had and we had a "pot luck" supper. Food and fun!

Pranks are normal in dorms. One night I came home from having closed a revival. Weary and tired, as I entered my room I heard a clock ticking. I did not have such! My clock was electric. I started searching. I found a clock and turned the alarm off. It was set for 1:00 a.m. I put it in the hall,

But the ticking continued! Before I was done there

were several clocks all set for a different time turned off and put in the hall, The next morning I never said a word but, got up and went about my business, Disappointed girls! The whole dorm was in on it and their plan had failed!

Dorm life has its benefits.. On other occasions I came in late to find my Hide-a-bed pulled out and my covers turned down and a little note wishing me a "good night."

Yet, it was special to move into my own home after living in a dorm for more than forty years. Mrs Esther Phiffer, a Methodist preacher's widow and a former missionary to Mexico, made possible my mobile home. The school built a roof over it and insulated. The carport and the patio was a gift from my friend,   Dr. Merry Scheflen.   Work teams as well as our KMHA workers added   to make this an enjoyable place to live.   After living in a "goldfish" bowl from age 18 to 68, I hardly knew how to cope with the "blessed quietness" of home.

I determine from the beginning that my home should be "a place of prayer" and a place where the Presence of God dwelt.

The Faculty /Staff (1951) included

Rev. Martha L. Archer (September 27, 1900 - September, 1988) Founder of KMBI, Academic Dean, Teacher (retired in 1975)

Dr Karl S. Paulo (March 3, 1993 - June 1981) Dean of Men. Teacher, Men's work supervisor; later became Academic Dean, and with Dr. McConnell's home going, the President of the KMHA.

Mrs. Nettie Myers (April 23, 1905 – November 8, 1880) Dean of Women, Teacher, Dorm Supervisor, Field Ministry Supervisor. (Retired 1979.)

Miss Celia Gibson (February 1894 – October 1978) Librarian, Teacher, Dorm Supervisor

Mrs Alice Fisher (September 25, 1915 – December 2011) Registrar. Teacher, Secretary to Academic Dean, Later Secretary to KMBC President

50

Miss Mildred Drake (August 1902 – November 1986)

  Choir and Chorus Director, Music Teacher (retired
  1974.)

Miss Henrietta M. Griffith (November 30, 1923 -)

  Teacher, Dorm Supervisor, Field Ministry Director,
  Alumni Editor, Alumni President (Retired May
  2013)

Mrs Ida Weber (June 8, 1877 – March 1, 1957)

  House-keeper, Ladies Work Supervisor

Miss Ruth Haan

  Cook and kitchen Work Supervisor

  OTHERS ADDED (1960 and later)

Gene Light- (April 2, 1948 – September 2013)

Carlene H. Light - (May 19, 1948 – March 3, 1911)

Mildred Anderson Allex - (April 14 1937 – September
  20, 1988)

Robert (Buddy) Allex - (December 8, 1933 February 1,
  2000)

Harold Davis - (August 11, 1905 - June 15, 2002)

Frances Elam Munson - (October 7, 1932 – April 9, 2007)

Hugh Munson – (September 12, 1929 – May 5, 2004)

Patsy Major - (March 12, 1934 – June 6, 2001)

MEMORIES CONCERNING A FEW CO-WORKERS

Through these 62 years of teaching I have been greatly blessed and influnced by my co-workers, at the beginning, all older; now, all younger.

REV. MARTHA L. ARCHER

Rev. Martha L. Archer was commissioned to start the Bible School in 1931. The story is told in Edith Vandewarker's book, <u>The Mountain Shall Be Thine</u>. I want to share just two memorizes concerning her.

Often she quoted her life verse. "The **meek** shall He guide in judgment, the **meek** will He teach His way." (Ps 25:9) **"It is not ye but the Holy Ghost."** (Mk 3:11)

Rev. Archer was a strong evangelist, leader, prayer warrior with her "fighting togs" on she wrestled until she had an answer. She challenged my prayer life.

We were in the fall convocation, October 1975. She was sick, weak and in pain. She told no one but continued to fulfill her responsibility as leader until the services ended. Many victories were won. Students and staff were built up in the faith. On Monday morning, October 1975, she was taken to the retirement home at Mt Carmel. She was never able to return to leadership. She spent her time in a tremendous prayer ministry for the schools and the KMHA churches. She went home to glory just before her 89th birthday in September 1988.

NETTIE HELWIG MYERS

Rev. and Mrs. Horace Myers were pastors ar the Index Community Church of KMHA when the Ky Mt Bible Institute began. Rev. Myers was asked to come teach. Nettie had three small children. She did not teach until after 1939 flash flood. That story is written in Bring My Sons From Far by Dr. Marie McCord, a niece.

RUTH HAAN

Ruth Haan, KMBI cook had an unusual story. Both

of her parents died very young leaving her to care for her siblings. She had not yet finished high school but she worked and cared for her brothers and sisters until they were through high school and college. Then at age 30, Ruth went to the local high school with all the "kids." She graduated and went to Chicago Evangelistic Institute. There she met Dr. McConnell. After graduation she came to KMBI to work in the kitchen.

As a child she had recived a missionary call. No board would accept her now at her age. She continued to serve at KMBI for many years. When she was in her fifties Rev. Doris Warren requested that she come to Bolivia and be her companion while the other missionaries were on furlough. Undaunted, Ruth raised the necessary money without even leaving KMBI campus. Friends heard and the money came. God blessed her ministry. She wrote back saying a smile is the same in any language. She learned a few Spanish words but never had trouble communicating. Love is easily translated.

ROBERT (BUDDY) AND MILDRED ALLEX

Mildred graduated from KMBI in 1958. She went to Good Samaritan Hospital Nursing School in Lexington, KY. After graduation she returned to KMBI and it was while nursing a student from Mt Carmel that she contracted encephalitis. She had a long hospital experience and was not expected to recover.

God answered with Isaiah 18:5 , "I have heard thy prayers and seen thy tears and will add fifteen years." God healed her in an amazing way. Mildred lived with Rev. H. Blaine West family and attended Short Street Wesleyan Church while recovering. She returned to KMBI and God led Robert Allex to join her. He was a licensed plumber and KMHA needed one.

God blessed their marriage with three children, Stella, Robert Jr, and Karl. All of them graduated from Mt Carmel and KMBC. Mildred and Buddy served many years at KMBC and KMHA.

HAROLD AND ELIZABETH THOMAS DAVIS

Rev. and Mrs Harold Davis came to minister in the KMHA in 1954, she as a teacher at Mt Carmel and he as a teacher at KMBI.

Harold Davis was a man of prayer, a Prayer Warrior, He spent many night hours quietly walking in his study interceeding for souls and situations. The Davis Prayer Chapel on campus is dedicated to his honor by former students and friends who financed its construction out of appreciation for his prayers.

His wholesome homespun humor livened his classes and helped his students remember lesson points. Here is a sample. In his southern Virgina accent, Rev Davis summorized the healing of the lame man. "In Acts 3 the lame man asked God for "alms" and received legs."

From his ministry and life experiences he encouraged students to live for Christ and others. Brother Davis was never critical or spoke unkindly about anyone. He spent his last years in a nursing home but continued a

56

ministry in prayer. He loved Jesus and people.

This poem was written by Harold on a flyleaf of his Bible;

My Prayer

Fire of God fall on me!

Flame of Heaven, illuminate me!

Let the Son of God shine on me,

Let the world see the God of all eternity.

Burning Bush, I take off my shoes,

And bow low before God, in Thee.

Oh, Thou, the great I AM, I adore Thee.

Oh, Truine God be all and all in me.

Oh,Holy Spirit, Flame of love connsume me-

Burn up all self and sin within me

Out of my ashes may, Thy glory shine

Thou canst see and Thou alone

Holy Spirit, from Father and Son

We honor Thee, for Thou alone

Canst glorify the Son and please the Father

through me

Out of my death to self comes life through Thee.

O Dove of Heaven, light upon me (Mt3:16)

May God the Son, do His work in me

Voice of Heaven, speak again thru me

May every soul through me see Thee

O Living Christ, Pure Joy, Holy Joy

May all see Thy joy in me

May every soul rejoice with me

And share this joy through all eternity.

H.J. Davis

GENE AND CARLENE HOLCOMB LIGHT

Gene and Carlene Holcomb Light are both graduates

of MtCarmel and KMBC . (1957 and 1959)   That

summer after graduation they were married and returned to work at KMBC that fall.

They were both soon involved in the work. Gene was men's work supervisor and very capable in carpentry, electrical work or whatever was needed. He was very efficient. Carlene supervised girls who worked in the laundry, In those early days we just had one washing machine. The laundry was done for the whole school. It was hung on the lines and each student claimed his/her own when it was dry. The school faculty/staff things were ironed and returned to owners under Carlene's supervision.

The Lights had five children- Laura, Tim, Daniel, Lynea and Craig. All graduated from Mt Carmel and KMBC. Carlene had several jobs after the children were in school, She cooked at Mt Carmel. Later she worked at WMTC Radio office. Her last and longest job was book keeper at KMBC. She also beautified the campus flower beds. Both Gene and Carlene had beautiful singing voices.

She especially sang or hummed much of the time. In 2012 She suffered a stroke from which she never fully recovered and was never able to speak. But she could sing along with those who visited with her.

In 2014 Gene stepped from a ladder into Heaven. His heart had given out, Today they are around the throne singing praises to the Lord.

HUGH AND FRANCES ELAM MUNSON

Hugh was a 1950 graduate of KMBI and stayed on as a maintenance worker for a while. Frances Elam was a student and they were dating. Soon after he and Frances married, they went to Asbury College for further education. They returned to pastor Tallega Church in Lee County.

As KMBI enlarged, another teacher was needed as well as a men's dorm supervisor. The Munsons were asked to come. Eventually Hugh felt the need to return to school to secure education in administration. He attended

Morehead and graduated with a Masters Degree. Frances served in several capacites including Dean of Women.

After Rev. Martha L. Archer retired (1975) Dr. J. Eldon Neihof became Academic Dean, serving until the death of Dr. Karl S. Paul (1980) KMHA President. Rev. Hugh Munson became KMBI's Academic Dean (1980). He served until his death in 2007.

MY OTHER MINISTRIES

Many summers I spent assisting in the churches making it possible for the pastors to have vacations. One summer Patsy Woodring and I spent time with Eunice Taulbee at Burning Fork. One major task of that summer was the building of a parsonage. The Prater Family, Robert, Alma and Fanny, had given land. Roy Turner was the builder. We all helped, even to the breaking up of rocks for the basement. We used the chimney rocks from the old Prater homestead. The Prater homestead if it could speak would tell many stories. It was a two story log

61

home built when this area was first settled. Peter Cart-wright, a circuit riding preacher, held services in this home. Fanny showed us a flat stone basin with a corn cob stopper. Circuit riders used it for hand washing. In the attic we found an old bear trap. The beds had rope "springs." The dining table was a large lazy-susan that seated up to 15 or more people. The center of it turned so you could help yourself to whatever you needed without disturbing anyone else. The floor was made from hand plane lumber. I thrilled to live in the midst of such history!

One summer I spent at Spencer Fork KMHA Church. As I preached, I noted that I had lost the attention of my whole group. I paused to ask what was going on. One boy pointed to the apple tree just outside the window. There was a snake! My text for that morning-- "Be wise as serpents and harmless as doves."(Matt 10:16) The Lord provided the object lesson as I preached.

Several summers I spent in Children's Ministry in

churches and camps. In the summer of 1970 I had a full schedule of meetings when Mrs Anne Scheflen asked me if I would like to go to Europe. "Of course," I said, never expecting to go. Mrs. Anne Scheflen told me to pray about it. She wanted me to go with her daughter, Merry, a Bolivian missionary who had not had a vacation for some eighteen years.

Merry and I had been fellow students and good friends at Asbury College years earlier. The trip included 10 counties of Europe and the Oberamagau Passion Play. I prayed and God gave me the verse, *"Sit still my daughter until thou see how the matter falls." (Ruth 3:18)* Within two weeks the word came that I was to go with all expenses paid. I quickly made arrangements for someone to do the youth camps and children's meetings. I secured my passport and was on my way.

The three week tour of Europe with Merry Scheflen was a delightful and one of God's special gifts to me. We rode on the crystal clear waters of the Amsterdam canals, cruised the Rhine River, had a gondola ride in the Venice canals, ate pizza Capparachi in an Italian restaurant, climbed the stairs where Martin Luther saw that we were justified by faith, saw the Swiss Alps, followed Jesus through the Passion week at Oberammergau. Time and space fail to tell the many places. I truly felt like one of God's "pets."

Revival work

I preached my very first revival at Yocum, KY. This was in the early 1950's. The pastor, Miss Wilbur, asked me to come. I was a teacher but God had also called me to preach. I put out a fleece and told God if He wanted me to preach more and hold occasional revivals that He would give us souls in this revival. One unusual victory came when an older lady sought and was gloriously saved. Her husband, a drunkard, had warned her that if she went forward he would beat her. She stepped out! He never did one thing. Later she was sanctified and became a pillar in her home church and community. Several others found real heart felt victory. I had God's answer!

Another early revival was at Bryant's Creek. The only way to the church at that time was to ford the Kentucky River or cross by means of a leaning half broken down swinging bridge. There was no electricity. We lighted the church by gasoline lanterns placed on shelves, one on each wall. A young teen age community boy had a vision of the church being filled and people outside looking in the windows. It came to pass! The lad was saved and a mother and daughter were saved early in the meeting. This stirred the devil. On the third or fourth night, the husband of the woman saved came to break up the meeting. He was drunk and staggered in and up to the front where I was preaching. He pointed his finger under my nose and said, "You don't belong here. You should be at home." Obviously he did not believe in women preachers. In fear I pointed him to Rev. Elijah Creech who with wisdom handled the situation and got him to leave. The revival continued. Others were saved including one young boy who now is a Gospel singer and leader for God. To God be the glory. I held other revivals here and in other states.

I served in several pastorates. In 1976 I began at Consolation Church. Consolation Church was located on Highway 192 half way between Hazel Green and Mize. When we went there, the church was about to close. God gave revival. New converts were radiant and happy. On one occasion, God urged me to go to a particular home. The man was hungering for salvation. We prayed as he sought God..   His wife was one of our members and was so delighted. We saw growth in the church and spiritual victories that were unusual.   In 1983, I felt God wanted me to give my final years to teaching. Little did I know that God had plans yet unknown to me.

Ministry in India

I received an invitation from the Wesleyan

missionaries to come to India. Carol Hart, a KMBI graduate, went with me. We planned to go between semesters rather than in the intense summer heat of India. We flew from New York December 13, 1985 and returned January 27, 1986. God quickened His Word to me.

"The Lord shall preserve thy going out and

thy coming in from this time forth and

forevermore" Psalm 121:8

"And ye shall not go out with haste, nor

by flight: for the Lord will go before you:

and the God of Israel will be thy,

rearward." Isa 52:12

Our itinerary included - village evangelism, leprosy hospital chapels, and revival, youth meetings, a pastor's holiness conference in Ragnangoan and in the Gujarat area. We visited the Methodist work in Calcutta, the World Gospel Mission work in Bangarapet and South India Bible Seminary. I felt this was all too big for me.

But I took off "my shoes" of inability and insufficiency when God spoke. *"As I was with Moses, so shall I be with thee, I will not leave thee nor forsake thee." (Joshua 1:5b)* When we arrived in India we saw a beautiful rainbow of promise in the sky and God gave us joy in seeing many victories.

My main ministry has been teaching in the Bible College. It is now 2017 as I write this. I am 93 years old. For the past few years I've taught a limited load. During 2013 I taught O. T. History and Survey of Holiness Literature, first semester; Pauline Epistles, second semester.

During September of 2009 Jack Neace, the Director of the Senior Citizen Center in Jackson, requested a Bible study. Each Tuesday morning I taught a Bible study to an eager group of senior citizens. The Bible study continued until 2013.

The school retirement gift was a cruise to Alaska Mary Ellen Mowery and I took this unusual cruise which included five Christian singing groups with concerts daily. It was a trip of a life time.

After having back surgery in August of 2013 I had a bad fall. I damaged my left leg. I could put no weight on it. I could not move it one inch. All the muscles and tendons were damaged. Following a time in the hospital and two and a half months in Beattyville Nursing Home for therapy I returned home.. Thanks to many prayers, perseverance and good therapy I now walk with a cane. And thanks to Mary Ellen who volunteered to live with me and help with my handicaps.

This story not quite complete-- KMBC built us a lovely spacious home that is fully handicap equipped.

Thus I close testifying – God has led, He has given "righteousness, joy and peace in the Holy Ghost." I wish that I could have done it all better. But to Him be all the praise and glory. With John Wesley I say, "Don't let me live to be idle or useless." And with Dyland Thomas, "Don't let me resign to age, let me keep ascending."

"OUT WITH JOY"

by

Henrietta M Griffith